7 Step Jumpstart to Becoming Your Best Self

7 Step Jumpstart to Becoming Your Best Self

2ND EDITION

ERICKA JOHNSON SETTLES

J MERRILL

J Merrill Publishing, Inc.
434 Hillpine Drive
Columbus, OH 43207
www.JMerrill.pub

Library of Congress Control Number: 2023901354
ISBN-13: 978-1-954414-74-7 (Paperback)
ISBN-13: 978-1-954414-73-0 (eBook)

Book Title: 7 Step Jumpstart to Becoming Your Best Self
Author: Ericka Johnson Settles

Contents

Acknowledgments

Special acknowledgment to my team who has supported me in every endeavor I've set out to do. To my mother, you have been my anchor and covered me with love and prayers. To my father, you've always told me I could accomplish anything I put my mind to. To my sister Adrienne, thank you for encouraging me to pursue my dreams. Finally, to my brother-in-law Kenny, your analytical eye has pushed me towards excellence.

To my extended family, thank you for promoting, encouraging, and supporting me unconditionally. To my besties, you have spoken life into me when the weight of the world was on my shoulders.

Last but not least, my heartbeats. To my favorite daughter, Naquia Chante, my manager, it will always be you and me. To my son, Wesley, my secret service detail, I love you to life. To my youngest son, Devon, my protector, continue to shine because you are a star. To Terrance, my life partner, companion, and friend, thank you will never be enough. You've been my rock, my stabilizer, and my biggest fan. Your unconditional love and support have been unwavering.

To the reader, thank you for taking this journey with me.

Foreword

This book is a wonderful tool to help you jump-start your new journey. The seven steps provided are each necessary for the change process. Yes, I said the two words individuals do not want to accept (change and process). Yet, these two words require something from you.

First, change requires work, dedication, and consistency. Secondly, the process requires some grit, commitment, and trust. Remember, you are the incentive! This is for you as you are most valuable, not your home, job, car, or money. You are certainly worth the work! Doing nothing is the easiest thing on this planet. It causes you to remain at the status quo; you can't grow in the status quo!

Your desire to change must be STRONGER than your desire to remain the same! How bad do you want it? Are you tired enough? Yes, your emotions will attempt to sabotage your success, but please do not allow your emotions and fears to bully or control you! You have something called a WILL. It wants to help you on this journey to jump-start your life.

Welcome your willpower, and validate your emotions, but for this trip, allow your willpower to remain in the driver's seat. You will notice a radical transformation if you stay the course. Read this book daily, and read it again, and again until it becomes a part of you. Change is hard but doable!

Kimberly Bozeman, MA.PCC Healthy Emotes Counseling

CHAPTER 1

Trust The Process

I n everything that we do, there is a process. Change, as inevitable as it may be, is a process. We often make numerous decisions in life that require us to alter some things. Now let's say, for the sake of argument, we are discussing paying off debt or starting a business. Whatever it may be, it takes a process to achieve. Before we go any further, what does the word process really mean? According to Merriam – Webster, process is defined as usually a fixed or ordered series of actions or events leading to a result; forward movement in time or place and: a natural phenomenon marked by gradual changes that lead toward a particular result.

The common denominator in each definition is movement. More specifically, forward movement is the most effective. Three things are imperative to accomplish any task. First, you must be determined to stay the course. Determine the purpose of the heart and mind to align with completing the goal.

Secondly, you must become disciplined. Discipline merely means being intentional with habitual acts to achieve the goal. Dedication is the final key. Be dedicated to the task and committed to accountability and transparency while having the willpower to stay the course.

You have to trust the process in order to reach the goal!

Identify what drives you most to accomplish a goal.

_____

_____

_____

What new habits have you acquired while working on this goal?

_____

_____

_____

Moment of Reflection

_____

_____

_____

AFFIRMATION

I must trust and believe in order to receive!!!

Trust the process even when it becomes uncomfortable, and YOU find yourself in unchartered territory. It's going to work in your favor.

CHAPTER 2

Don't stop when you're tired. Stop when you're finished

Have you ever started a project that never got completed? Think about it - You had a brilliant idea to do something, make something, or write something. Go full steam ahead by getting things in place. Not to mention the time you tried losing weight. You were eating salads, drinking water, and giving up everything that tasted good. You were even getting up every morning and going to the gym. You did your best to get fit but only to lose 2 pounds. Finally, you tire of doing the same thing without the expected results. So, you just quit.

Maybe you started school, got through your first three quarters, and suddenly got sick or lost a job. Now that things have gotten back in order, you keep putting off returning to school, quarter after quarter. Eventually, you give up. Quitting is not an option. You have to get back in the race.

A scripture says, "the race isn't given to the swift but the one who endures till the end."

You must learn to endure the tests and trials of life. What does endurance look like? Sometimes, it's wearing a smile when crying is an appropriate response. Push through the doubt, discouragement, and disappointment to show up for yourself. Be determined that nothing or no one can stop you from accomplishing what you set out to do.

Most importantly, keep a mental picture of yourself walking in your destiny. You have to see it before you can see it. I am reminded of the story of a boy who had a difficult childhood filled with abuse at the hands of his father. This teenager even attempted suicide to escape his life. At 16, this young man changed his first name to separate himself from his abuser.

Though he had dropped out of school, this young man later got his GED. One day while watching Oprah Winfrey, he was inspired to write about his life experiences. As he found his passion in writing, he saved $12,000 for his first production. Unfortunately, his debut production only had a disappointing 30 people.

Pursuing his passion, he lived out of his car, continuing to work at his craft by participating in many productions. He never stopped writing. Six years later, he made another attempt at Theater audiences. To his surprise, it was a sellout event. He finally earned critical acclaim as well as commercial success. Tyler Perry is a world-renowned producer, director, actor, screenwriter, playwright, author, songwriter, entrepreneur, and philanthropist. You may not be Tyler Perry, Oprah Winfrey, Beyoncé, or Barack Obama. Still, you are just as important as they are. So let your passion fuel your pursuit and walk in your Purpose. Remember, don't stop when you're tired; stop when you're finished.

What is your plan for success?

_____

_____

_____

Write down your single biggest challenge. Now write what you would say to someone in the same situation.

_____

_____

_____

Moment of reflection.

_____

_____

_____

AFFIRMATION

The race isn't given to the swift but to the one who endures to the end.

I have to show up for myself even when no one else does.

CHAPTER 3

Self-Confidence

Let's talk about self-confidence. That is something that a lot of people do not possess. Then others confuse confidence with pride. Self-confidence is a belief in oneself and one's ability to succeed. Now that you understand self-confidence let's explore some things that hinder you from living with self-confidence. Comparison is one of the biggest things to block self-confidence. Stop comparing yourself to others and their expectations. Everyone is uniquely made with their own identity, gifts, and talents.

Let me break this down differently. The human body has many organs, limbs, bones, and muscles. The eyes cannot compare to the nose or hands. They don't serve the same purpose or function.

Secondly, stop complaining. Research has shown that complaining shrinks the hippocampus - an area of the brain that is critical to problem-solving and intelligent thoughts. Your thought process begins to rewire. Need I say more? Stop complaining!! Finally, kill the noise of criticism. What do I mean by that? Stop listening to the naysayers, critics, and haters. Those who have never attempted what you have decided to do find it necessary to comment, condemn, or criticize your efforts. For those in the faith community, there is a familiar story but to everyone else, let me take the time to share it with you. Matthew 14:24 (KJV) is where we picked up on the story.

Later that night, the boat had drifted a long distance from the shore by the wind and waves. The disciple noticed an image, or possibly a ghost walking towards them, and they were filled with fear. Finally, Peter had the courage to speak to Jesus. "Lord, if it's you, tell me to come to you on the water." Peter began to walk on water, something the others never had the courage to do. Like I said, kill the noise of criticism and judgment from others who are overcome with fear and doubt.

Once you've stopped the comparison, and complaining, and ignored the criticism, begin looking at ways to build self-confidence. A simple but vital step to building self-confidence is taking the time to *recognize* every win, no matter how big or small. Doing so will allow you to *realize* that your only competition is with yourself. Then, continue that work to *reach* that next level. Every day speak with positive affirmations and declarative statements.

Taking an aggressive approach in canceling the limited beliefs to unlimited potential and opportunities. Keep in mind, "All things are possible."

How has this lack of confidence affected your life?

_____

_____

_____

What is your limited belief? Write a declarative statement as a response to this belief.

_____

_____

_____

Moment of Reflection

_____

_____

_____

AFFIRMATION

I am becoming the best version of myself!!!

IF YOU CANNOT BELIEVE IN WHO YOU ARE, BELIEVE IN WHO YOU ARE BECOMING.

CHAPTER 4

Your Words Have Power

Growing up, there was a saying, "Sticks and stones may break your bones, but words will never hurt you." Now that was a lie if a lie was ever told. The Bible says, "life and death are in the power of the tongue, and those who love it will eat its fruit." Words have an undeniable force to heal, hurt, help, hold, humiliate, honor, and humble. There is forcible energy that is produced by the magnitude of the language that we use. What does that look like, you ask?

The energy you feel is often transferred in how you communicate with and about others. As stated in the previous chapter, research has shown that complaining shrinks the hippocampus – an area critical to problem-solving and intelligent thoughts. As a result, your thought process begins to rewire. The way you communicate will contribute to your brain's functioning. This can be said; your words are a signal to your brain to strengthen or weaken the functioning of the brain.

So, let me encourage you as I encourage myself, watch the words that come out of your mouth. You could be killing yourself, your family, your finances, and your future. Ask yourself, are my words helpful or harmful? Will the language I use heal or hurt? Will the listener be honored or humiliated by what they heard? Whenever I address an issue with an individual, I am taught to use the sandwich method.

The sandwich method is three simple steps. First, begin with a positive affirmation/confirmation to set the tone of empathy. Second, address the problem with care and concern in a non-judgmental way. Third, end the conversation on a positive attribute of that individual.

I will end with this: Your words have power but are empowering.

Take a moment to recall your last conversation with a loved one. What did your words produce?

_____

_____

_____

How can I use my words to heal even when I am hurting?

_____

_____

_____

Moment of reflection.

_____

_____

_____

AFFIRMATION

I will use my Words to empower, equip and encourage myself and others for the greater good.

"**Let no corrupt communication proceed out of your mouth, but that which is good to the use of edifying, that it may minister grace unto the hearers.**"

— EPHESIANS 4:29 KJV

CHAPTER 5
Self Sabotage

S elf-sabotage is defined as the act of destroying or damaging something deliberately so that it does not work correctly. It takes root in our minds out of fear or rejection. Often, rejection or fear can be traced to a traumatic encounter where you were abandoned, deserted, forgotten, forsaken, ignored, neglected, or refused. From that moment, our thoughts watered the seeds of the heinous act.

Your thoughts become your words. Your words become your actions; your actions become your habits. Your habits become your character. Your character becomes your destiny. You are just living in a vicious cycle of self-inflicted betrayal. Giving life to feeling not being good enough, smart enough, pretty enough, or having what it takes. I can recall when my husband and I were going through a rough patch and decided to close our business. I often came home from work afraid and uncertain but never expressed it. In all actuality, I did the exact opposite.

I pretended to be ok and started nitpicking on everything that he said or did. This would continue until things escalated into an altercation. At that moment, I could deflect things that were not even relevant— inadvertently destroying the foundation of the relationship. I just wanted to be held and told it would be ok. Instead of being transparent about my feelings, I created an environment of chaos because I was afraid.

Then one day in prayer, I was reminded of my actions. I rewound the response and, at that point, could recognize the cause and effects of my life. I could see the cycles of self-sabotage. Moving forward, it brought about an awareness of my feeling of fear. I intentionally disrupted the pattern and found the courage to swap my fears for faith. Faith in accepting things may not change, finding the power to move forward, and modeling the rejection of every self-depleting fearful thought.

Take a moment to write down when you have experienced fear or rejection. Explore what the root was.

_____

_____

_____

What are some things you can do differently to yield different results?

_____

_____

_____

Moment of reflection.

_____

_____

_____

AFFIRMATION

Today I exchange my fear and rejection for faith and acceptance.

Prayer for Serenity

God, grant me the serenity to accept the things I cannot change, the courage to change the things I can, and the wisdom to know the difference.

Living one day at a time, enjoying one moment at a time; accepting hardship as a pathway to peace; taking, as Jesus did, this sinful world as it is, not as I would have it; trusting that You will make all things right if I surrender to Your will; so that I may be reasonably happy in this life and supremely happy with You forever in the next.

Amen.

CHAPTER 6

Recalibrate Your Focus

Focusing on what's going wrong or who did us wrong is easy. I believe it's in our innate thoughts to hold on to something so long until we succumb to only seeing the wrong. The saying is, "You can't see the forest for the trees." The trees in your life may represent the loss of a job, illness, separation, financial devastation, and loss of a loved one or a relationship. But remember, it's not the whole picture of your life, but merely a snapshot of all your experiences.

Let's break this down to get a better understanding. A forest is an ecosystem's term characterized by the dominance of tree cover. They contain a variety of masses, like many other organisms. However, they differ in composition and structure, being layers in the forest. These are both affected by biotic and abiotic factors. The biotic factors are humans, animals, and plants. The abiotic factors are soil, moisture, sunlight, and climate.

Please stay with me; I'm going somewhere with this. A mature forest is made up of structural layers. The overstory comprises the crowns of the uppermost trees in the forest. The understory is made up of the crowns of shorter forest trees and includes the shrub layer. The forb layer is made up of non-woody plants. Finally, the litter layer includes leaves, branches, and other debris that have fallen onto the forest floor. Each layer adds dimensions and offers diversity. Understanding what layers exist helps us understand how forests function.

In plain English, your challenges symbolize the uppermost trees in the forest. Though big, tall, and deeply rooted, they are stationary. You can walk around them, climb over them, cut them down, or admire what grows on them. You can also embrace the growth, character, resilience, patience, and wisdom they produce. So stop focusing on your pain, problems, and predicament. But adjust your focus to your purpose, passion, and promise.

What does each tree represent?

_____

_____

_____

What is your forest producing?

_____

_____

_____

Moment of reflection.

_____

_____

_____

AFFIRMATION

I walk by faith, not sight, allowing hope to guide me.

When looking through the optical lens of your life, do you see an obstacle or an opportunity?

CHAPTER 7

Authenticity

I'll begin this closing chapter with a question.

Are you living in true authenticity? What does it mean to be authentic? Authenticity is defined as being genuine, representing one's true nature or beliefs. I know there are times when I haven't been true to myself or anyone else—pretending to be or do something with the hope of acceptance, approval, or affirmation from others. I know you can relate to this. It could be something as simple as the clothes you wear, styling your hair, talking a certain way, and doing things to fit in. Let me ask another question, have you ever made a decision based on what you felt would be socially acceptable?

Can I be transparent? I have for a significant part of my life. I remember growing up with a sister who sang in a group that traveled abroad and was well sought after. During those years, I had the opportunity to sing for my family at events or church. In those moments, I always compared my abilities to my sister. I would hear, "Now she can sing pretty well, but her sister can really sang." Imagine the internal struggle always to attempt to measure up to the standard set by someone's preference. This judgment and level of criticism became crippling in the growth of becoming my true self and being authentic. I often attempted to sing by mimicking those esteemed by others, leaving me feeling inadequate and insufficient. Then one day, while publicly singing, I heard a sound different than anything I had ever heard. The sound was smooth, well-balanced, and captivating. To my surprise, it was my voice. I had been looking for it most of my life. The voice I had been searching for was there all along.

I could not hear it because I was busy listening to the opinions of others. Jill Scott gave an interview that embodied the essence of authenticity. She was asked about being nervous performing following Erykah Badu. She responded by stating, "We all have our own thing. That's magic: everybody comes with their own sense of strength and their own queendom. Mine could never compare to hers, and hers could never compare to mine." Learning to embrace every moment and live in the beauty of your true self embodies authenticity. William Shakespeare penned the famous quote, "This above all, to thine own self be true." So, take a moment and begin writing the next chapter of your life with your truth and authenticity.

List something that sets you apart from everyone else.

_____

_____

_____

Do you recognize the person looking back at you when looking in the mirror?

_____

_____

_____

Moment of reflection.

_____

_____

_____

AFFIRMATION

I WILL BE MY BEST SELF, UNAPOLOGETICALLY

Don't be afraid to be YOU. Someone is waiting to love YOU, celebrate YOU, and embrace YOU.

NEXT STEPS

Now that you have come to the end of this journey, you may ask, "What's Next"?

Reread this book, and I am confident you will get a new perspective each and every time. Every day we get a chance to do this thing called life.

Never stop learning and loving YOU!

About the Author

Growing up, Ericka often joined her mother in evangelist ministry by the visitation of homebound members, feeding the less fortunate, and singing to those who listened. Thus, a seed of compassion was planted and began to grow.

Facing and overcoming challenges of childhood trauma, becoming a teenage mother, and a failed marriage, Ericka has been able to use each obstacle as a driving force to become more resilient and serve others.

"Ericka J Is Me" is the launch pad for healing, restoration, and fulfillment. Ericka uses her voice to empower, encourage and equip others to become their best self. She recently adopted the motto, "I have to show up for me!" In her day-to-day interactions as a Substance Use Disorder Therapist, Ericka inspires others to reach for their goals and to conquer what seems impossible.

Ericka, an Ohio native, is a mother of three adult children, a loving wife, an entrepreneur, a Licensed Chemical Dependency Counselor Assistant, a Certified Life Coach, Speaker, Vlogger/Blogger, Psalmist, and National Recording Artist. In addition, she has released several musical projects that can be found on all digital media outlets.

Ericka is a tenacious woman that never gives up, pursuing her purpose and passion.

CONNECT WITH THE AUTHOR

Visit https://www.erickajisme.com and subscribe to get updates, access exclusive sales, and stay

 facebook.com/erickajisme
instagram.com/erickajisme

www.ingramcontent.com/pod-product-compliance
Lightning Source LLC
Chambersburg PA
CBHW070946120626
46546CB00004B/1594